AF251907

EMBARKING 1 ON 1 GUIDE

INTRODUCTION

Think of a time when you embarked on a journey: a vacation, camping trip, move to a new home, start of a new job . . . you fill in the blank. What were you feeling? Anxious? Excited? Maybe a little of both?

As you open this guide, you're embarking on a similar journey, but this one is an expedition into authentic, godly manhood. As you begin, you may experience similar emotions as you would with anything else that's new. This may feel like a journey into the unknown, but as you'll soon discover, it may be one of the best decisions you've ever made, and you can trust your Guide.

WHO IS THIS GUIDE DESIGNED FOR? (AND WHAT IF I'M NOT THE BIOLOGICAL DAD?)

This Guide is designed for dads and their sons, but it's also for stepfathers, grandfathers, uncles, godfathers/guardians, coaches, teachers, small group leaders, or any other man who takes on the role of "dad" in a boy's life. (This Guide will use the terminology of "dad" and "son" to keep things simple.) Regardless of your title, thank you for stepping into this vital role in a young man's life. You have the incredible privilege of discipling this boy into a godly man. And, by the way, this Manhood Journey is for you, too! As you walk this trail together, you will discover and grow as an authentic man yourself.

If you are standing in as the father figure, the apostle Paul can be a good role model for you. He called Timothy, a young man he met on his missionary travels, his "true son in the faith" (1 Timothy 1:2). Look through 1 and 2 Timothy and watch for how Paul developed his son in the faith as a godly man and servant leader.

WHAT IF I'M USING THIS GUIDE WITH MORE THAN ONE BOY?

You can use this Guide with several boys at once, but it's designed to be used in a very small grouping of about two to four. One of the main purposes is to get to know your son(s) and have personal discussions with him. Manhood Journey also has studies for small groups of men and their sons, available at www.manhoodjourney.org.

CAN WE USE THIS GUIDE IF WE'RE NOT INVOLVED IN A MANHOOD JOURNEY SMALL GROUP?

Yes! While the small group program and the Guides work well together, you can meet with your son and use this guide separately from the group experience. Just skip any parts that refer directly to the group meetings (the "Group Session Review" section, for instance).

HOW CAN WE LEARN ABOUT, FIND, OR START A MANHOOD JOURNEY SMALL GROUP?

You can start or join an existing Manhood Journey small group with other men and their sons. Go to www.manhoodjourney.org to learn more, get started, or order your studies. The website even includes an interactive basic training for leaders.

The Manhood Journey small group program is a non-denominational, Bible-based approach to building young men through the discipleship and mentorship of fathers. It features guided Biblical discussion with hands-on, interactive activities. Groups consist of six to eight dads, who each bring their son(s). Young men without an engaged dad can be brought by a caring man who wants to pour into their life. Groups meet in six-week sprints at a church or someone's home with discussions guided by modules that cover various topics. The young men are normally between the ages of 8 and 17.

HOW DO I USE THIS GUIDE?

This guide is designed to provide you with ideas and a basic structure for spending time with and having meaningful conversations with your son. Some values that will help:

• Don't think of these sessions so much as "lesson plans," although you are in a position of "teacher" by being a good model for your son. Look at this book as a guide for you and your son to engage in discussions about godly manhood together.

• Each session purposely contains more content than you need. You know your son better than those who put this guide together. Use the ideas, discussions, and questions that best work for you and your son based on his age, personality, temperament, and understanding.

• Each session begins with "A Word to Dad" to help you think through the issues before you get together with your son. This opening page will encourage you in your vital role as a father.

• Each session is divided into four main sections:

1. BUILDING Our Relationship

A time for dad and son to review the group time and warm up for the day's topic. You'll begin your time with your son(s) by creating a "porch moment" together. Think of The Andy Griffith Show, when Andy and Opie would sit and chat on their front porch in Mayberry. Andy asked questions of his son and then listened well to his responses. They talked about what was going on in Opie's world, a world of schoolwork, sports, piano lessons, best friends, bullies, and girlfriends. Andy had a window into his son's world because of these times spent talking.

2. KNOWING God's Word

An opportunity to read, memorize, study, and apply the Bible to real, everyday life.

3. SERVING Others

This is the "so what" part. You will talk about how to put what you're learning into action to make an impact on others.

4. TALKING with God

You will close each time with your son with a brief time of prayer, simply talking with God about what you are learning and praying for your son(s).

•Have fun! Enjoy these valuable moments together with your son.

FIVE VITAL PRINCIPLES
TO MAKE YOUR TIME WITH YOUR SON VALUABLE AND FRUITFUL

1. Take ownership of the process. In Ephesians 6:4, God's Word instructs fathers to bring up our children "in the training and instruction of the Lord." The Message translation says it even more directly: "Take them by the hand and lead them in the way of the Master." Dad, don't leave this to chance; bringing up sons to become godly men will not happen on its own. So initiate. Be strong and courageous. Be a man of action!

2. Be humble, honest, and helpful in all your conversations. The goal is authentic, godly manhood, so lead the way by being real, but only in ways that are beneficial to your son.

Be prepared to share areas where you struggle in your faith and pursuit of being a godly man. Let your son see that you are a man who needs God's grace as you work toward godliness.

3. Engage in conversations, not lectures. *Try not to give pat answers or solve your son's problems. Rather, talk out the issues and help him come to the answers on his own, with your guidance. Remember that more is caught than taught. If your son asks for your opinion, however, don't be afraid to give it as part of the discussion. Most importantly, take your questions to God, seeking wisdom from his Word. This Guide will help you do that.*

4. Give attention to learning about your son. *A major objective is to know his heart, which means you will need to unpeel numerous layers over the upcoming weeks. Ask questions. Use the discussion questions in this guide, but often the best discussions happen through the follow-up questions you ask that aren't in this guide. Then—and this critical!—listen. Listen not only to his words but also pay attention to his body language, tone of voice, and emotion. Here's another practical piece of advice: Put your cell phone or other electronic gadget away during your discussions. Let your son know he has your undivided attention while you meet together.*

5. Apply biblical wisdom to real life. *The Bible provides the answers to our questions. It is God's instruction book for our lives, and it is useful for teaching, rebuking, correcting, and training in righteousness (2 Tim. 3:16). Throughout these sessions, you will dig into the Scriptures as your primary source of wisdom.*

HOW MUCH TIME WILL EACH SESSION TAKE?

The easy answer to this question is, "as long as it takes"! Time frames for each activity are purposely not included because one of the main goals of these Guides is to help you hang out with and talk with your son rather than work through a set, rigid agenda. These discussions can take approximately 45-60 minutes, but that time frame doesn't account for tossing ball, shooting baskets, and extended discussions. Try not to constantly look at your watch! If that might be a temptation, take it off and leave it on your nightstand.

You will be encouraged to build each session around activities your son and you enjoy. Take advantage of the time you have together to build memories as you build up your son.

WHAT OTHER SUPPLIES DO I NEED FOR THIS JOURNEY?

• The most important thing you need as you embark on this journey is a willing heart, a desire for your son to become a godly man.

• Be sure to have a Manhood Journey Notebook for yourself and each son who is participating. You will use these notebooks in these six sessions for note taking, illustrations, and more. Also, these notebooks will become like journals of your journey together. They will become keepsakes for both of you, like commemorative markers along the trail that will remind you in years to come of what God was doing in your life at this point in the journey.

• *You and your son should each have your own Bible, whether it's a traditional printed Bible or a Bible app on your phone or other electronic device. Some shorter Scripture passages will be provided in this guide, but for most of the main passages, only references will be given. It's extremely valuable for you and your son to look these up in your Bibles.*

• *We have many other tools available for you. Find them on our website at www.manhoodjourney.org. There you'll find resources, blog posts, training, information about retreats, and much more.*

🐦 **@manhoodjourney**   **f** **facebook.com/manhoodjourney**

"So commit yourselves wholeheartedly to these words of mine. . . . Teach them to your children. Talk about them when you are at home and when you are on the road, when you are going to bed and when you are getting up." —Deuteronomy 11:18-19

EMBARKING
WEEK 1

THE BIG ROCKS

A WORD TO DAD

It is a high honor and privilege to be a dad! You are taking your responsibility seriously by being involved in this Manhood Journey with your son(s). Remember that you are not alone. Many other dads are taking this journey along with you, so depend on one another as you hike this trail. You also have a heavenly Father who is walking with you. He is your strength, your trail guide along the way. He knows this trail better than anyone because he created it.

You are embarking on a vital journey together on the trail to becoming godly men. Before meeting together with your son(s), spend some time alone with your heavenly Father. Ask him to give you the understanding, love, patience, wisdom, and words you need as you build a godly relationship with your son. Your Father has all the resources you need. Take a few moments to humbly allow him to pour everything into you that you need to be a godly dad for your son. Then you can simply overflow into your son what your Father has poured into you.

Before you begin your "meeting" with your son, ask him some open questions such as this:

What's one good thing going on at school [or on a sports team, with an interest, hobby, or activity, with your friends, etc.]?

Then just listen and ask follow-up questions.

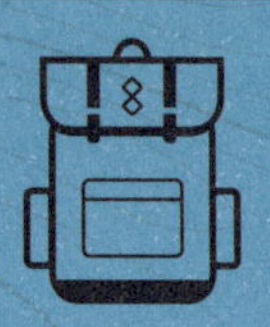

BUILDING
OUR RELATIONSHIP
EMBARKING 1 ON 1 GUIDE

GROUP SESSION REVIEW

Engage your son(s) in a dialogue about the meeting using any of the following questions as you see fit.

- What did you think about our first meeting together?

- What was your favorite thing about it?

- What did you think about the illustration with the rocks?

- What did you learn?

- Did you have any questions or thoughts that you didn't have a chance to bring up (or didn't want to talk about) at the meeting?

BE AN ACTIVE LISTENER

1. Look at your son as he speaks,
keeping your body posture open and receiving.

2. Nod your head or use other nonverbal and
verbal responses so he knows you're hearing him.

3. Try not to interrupt.

4. Ask follow-up questions.

5. Remember that the purpose for the questions in
this guide is to initiate discussion, not give a test!

THE FIVE "BIG ROCKS"

Let's work on memorizing the Five Big Rocks.
A godly man . . .

1. **TRUSTS** God
2. **KNOWS** his Word
3. **PRAYS** fervently
4. **BUILDS** relationships
5. **SERVES** others

SAY

As with most things in life, it's important for you, Dad, to go first. That doesn't mean, however, that you must have these memorized beforehand. It means that you model the value of knowing these Big Rocks and working on this project together. Don't be surprised, in fact, if your son is able to memorize these faster than you!

There are many different memorization techniques you could use. Here are two ideas. Use whatever works best for your son.

• Write each "Big Rock" on a literal large rock from your yard. Different sizes, colors, and shapes will aid in the memorization. Put the rocks out of sight and then pull one out and see if your son can name the "Big Rock" without seeing the words.

•On a page in each of your Manhood Journey Notebooks, draw a map. Think of each Rock as a stopping point along your trail. So for instance, your first stop is at "Trust God." Then make connections between that stop and the next one: In order to trust God, we need to "Know his Word," and so forth.

Talk about what other rocks you would each add to this list. Dad, you go first. So for instance, you might add, "Takes care of his family" or "works hard." Encourage your son to tell you what he would add to these. Be sure to affirm your son's ideas; let him know you appreciate him and what he has to say. Tell him you're proud of him for what he prioritizes. Add these to your Manhood Journey Notebooks.

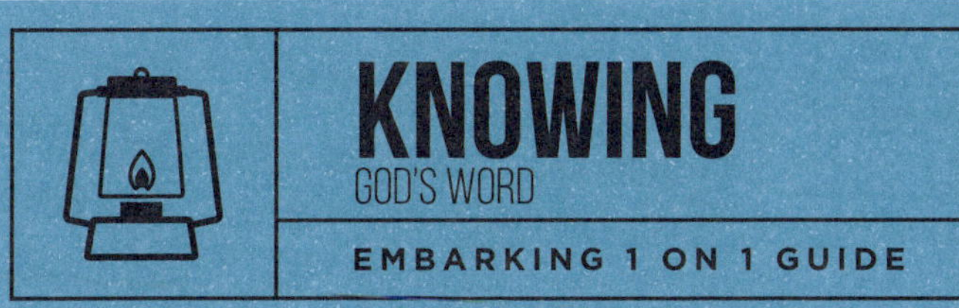

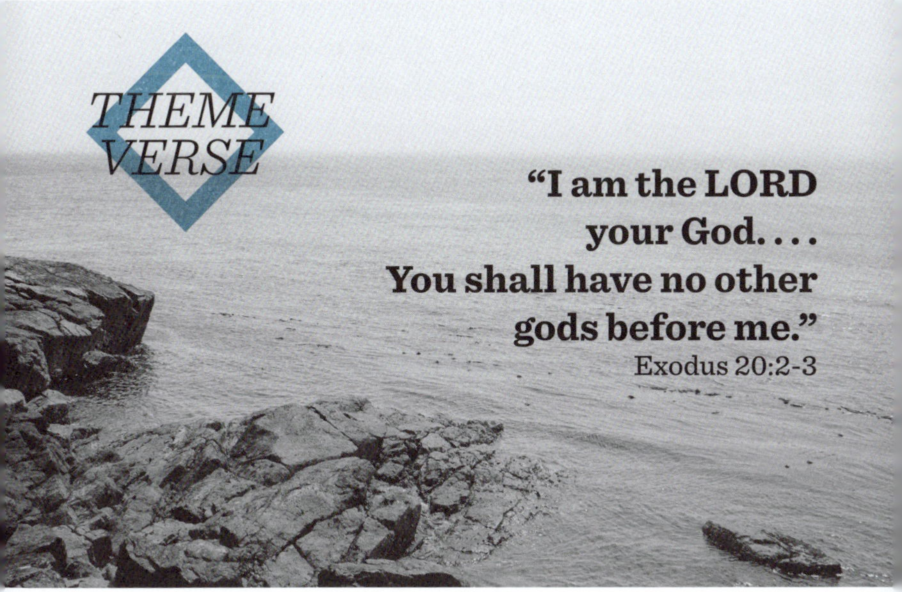

THEME VERSE

"I am the LORD
your God....
You shall have no other
gods before me."
Exodus 20:2-3

Write this verse at the top of a new page in each of your Manhood Journey Notebooks.

SAY

The very first of the Ten Commandments God gave us was that we put him first, above everything and everyone else. When we get things out of order and make other things or other people more important than God, we make those things false gods or idols. Everything else depends on putting God first in our lives, loving and trusting him.

Go over this verse several times with your son. See if your son can remember it. In future weeks you'll spend more time on memorizing the theme verse, but since you've already worked on memorizing the "Big Rocks," don't spend too much time on this here. It's far more important that you understand the vitality of putting God first in your lives than memorizing it.

The theme verse is a foundation for the rest of our Bible study. Each of the other verses we'll look at will reinforce and provide more specific ideas for how to live out the theme verse.

- Try to engage your son as much as possible in this discussion.

- As always, it's vital for you to be humble, honest, and helpful with your son.

- For each question, prayerfully decide if you should respond first or let your son initiate.

- You should share, not just ask questions. Remember, this is a dialogue!

Read or ask your son to read Matthew 22:36-40.

Which of the Five Rocks does this passage involve?

Your son may immediately say #1: Trusts God, which is right, but keep digging. Ask how the others Big Rocks relate to the passage:

- *How might "knowing God's Word" help us to love God more (especially with our minds)?*

- *How can praying fervently help us to build our relationship with God?*

- *How are Rocks 4 and 5 related to loving others as ourselves?*

Why do you think these two commands, to love God and others, are the "greatest" of all of God's commands?

Jesus was putting a priority on relationships. They are more important than money or possessions or anything else in the world. If we get these two commands right, we'll get everything else right.

If tomorrow you were to love God with all your heart, soul, mind, and strength—in other words, with everything you've got—what specifically would that look like? What would you do differently?

This is a good opportunity to honestly and humbly share an area where you find yourself struggling to love God with everything. Share only what would be helpful for your son, so that he can see that you're working on your own relationship with God. Be transparent and positive.

Read or ask your son to read Matthew 6:31-34.

Background*: Jesus had been teaching the people not to worry so much about all the things they need and want in life. Instead they should trust God. Pagans are people who don't believe in God. "Righteousness" simply means living rightly for God— doing things his way, obeying him, and trusting him. Focus your discussion around verse 33.*

What comes into your mind when you think of a "kingdom"?

Your son may say a lot of things here. You might ask and discuss books or movies (i.e., The Lion King; The Princess Bride; Robin Hood; The Lion, the Witch, and the Wardrobe; The Lord of the Rings) that include kings, heroes, and battles.

If your son is young, ask him to draw a picture of what he imagines a kingdom looks like in his Manhood Journey Notebook. Then ask him questions about his picture. What's happening? Who's the hero? Who's the king? What do the subjects of a good king do?

A kingdom means there's a king!

What was Jesus saying should be our very first priority?

If God is the king and we live in his kingdom, how should we respond when he gives us a mission and directions?

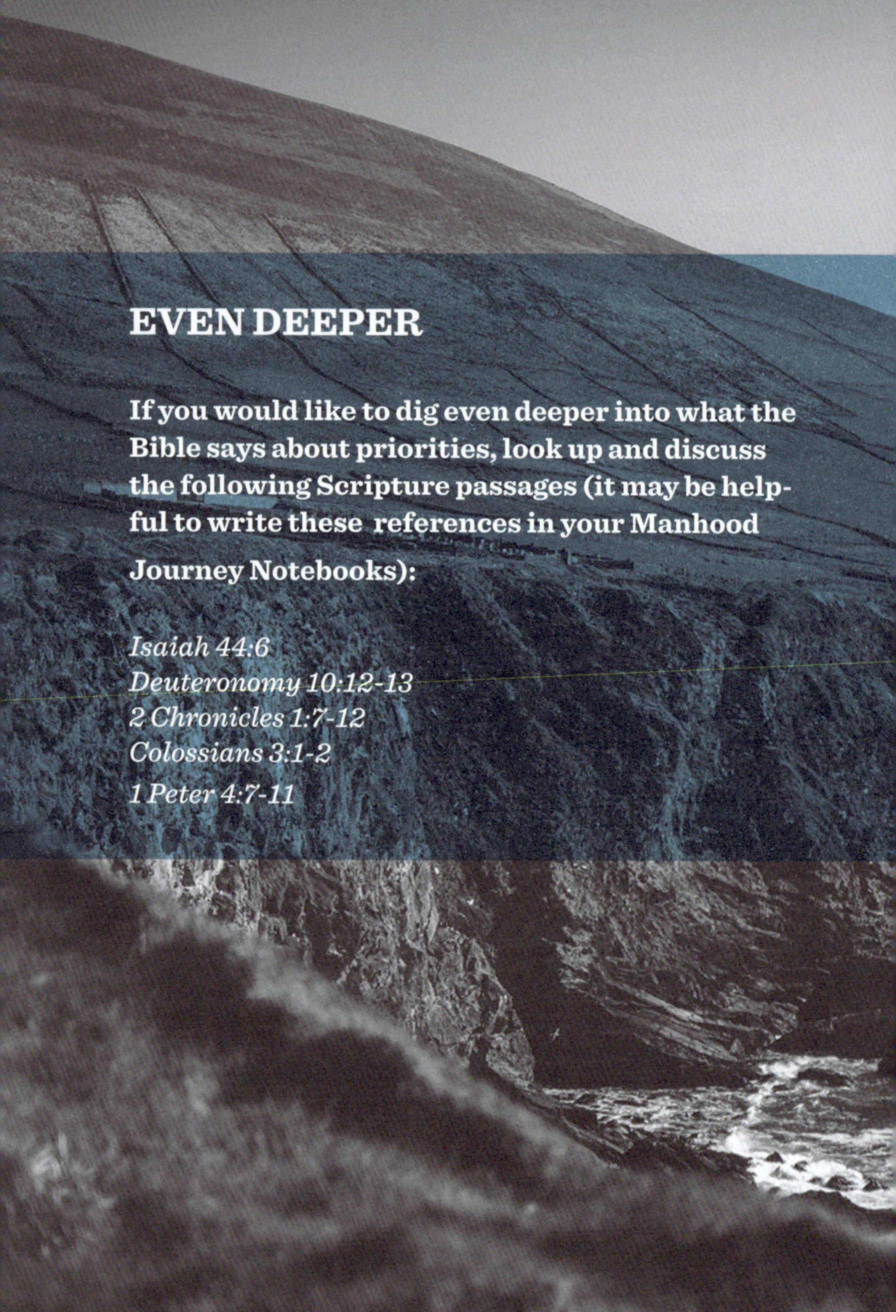

EVEN DEEPER

If you would like to dig even deeper into what the Bible says about priorities, look up and discuss the following Scripture passages (it may be helpful to write these references in your Manhood Journey Notebooks):

Isaiah 44:6
Deuteronomy 10:12-13
2 Chronicles 1:7-12
Colossians 3:1-2
1 Peter 4:7-11

SAY

Serving others is a vital part of our journey together. When we serve others we put into action what God is doing in our lives. After all, a godly man serves others! He makes an impact on the people around him.

So let's talk about how we can make serving other people a priority in our lives. Jesus is our best example.

Read or ask your son to read Mark 10:45.

**How can you make it a priority
this week to love and serve another person?**

This can be something relatively small such as taking out the garbage without being asked, cleaning up his room, or letting his sister have first choice as to where to sit in the car, for instance. The big idea here is to simply see putting others first and serving them as a "Big Rock" in your lives, a way of trusting and obeying God.

Remember to share with your son what you will do this week to serve another person as well.

**This commitment to serve others is just between
you and me. It's our secret, OK? We're serving
not to get the applause of others but simply to do
what a godly man does.**

Whatever you choose to do, write it in your own Manhood Journey Notebook.

TALKING
WITH GOD

EMBARKING 1 ON 1 GUIDE

Close your time by praying for your son. Make this a very simple prayer, something such as this:

SAY

God, thanks for the time my son and I have spent together today. You know how proud I am of him and how much I love him. Please give us your strength to live for you first the rest of this week. Amen.

EMBARKING
WEEK 2
SETTING OUT ON
THE JOURNEY

A WORD TO DAD

Have you considered lately what a privilege and responsibility you have as a dad? Everyone wants to make an impact and leave a legacy through his life, and that's exactly what you get to do as you spend time with your son(s) as part of this Manhood Journey.

But there's even more to it! The Bible promises that "a good man leaves an inheritance to his children's children" (Prov. 13:22). Your son may still be a child, yet the time you invest into him today will affect his children!

As you prepare to meet with your son, respond in your Manhood Journey Notebook to the following questions.

What thoughts do you need to change so you can reap a destiny that leaves an inheritance for your children's children?

What thoughts do you need to plant in your son so he can leave a legacy, too?

Before meeting with your son, spend some time doing something he enjoys: tossing ball, shooting baskets, kicking around a soccer ball, or playing a game of chess or a video game, for instance. Use that time to create your "porch moment," asking him some questions about his week, school, friends, and so forth.

Follow up with your son from your discussion last week. Tell him what you did to prioritize loving God and others. Tell him specifically what you did to love and serve another person anonymously. Then ask him what he did to keep God and others his top priorities. Ask what he did to serve another person.

GROUP SESSION REVIEW

Use any of these questions as you see fit.

- How do you think our group meeting went?
- What did you like most about the meeting?
- What did you learn?
- How is becoming a man like a journey?
- When do you think that journey ends? At age 16? 18? 21? 85? (Be sure to share what you think, Dad!)
- Did you have any questions or thoughts during the meeting that you didn't want to ask or talk about at the time? If so, what are they?

Also, consider some of the discussions during the meeting that stood out to you. Share what you were thinking or feeling, or ask your son what he thought. For instance, one of the questions was, "Sons, what are some things about your dad that you'd like to be able to model yourself after?" If his response made you proud, tell him so!

On the "Word to Dad" page, you were asked to respond to two questions in your Manhood Journey Notebook. Prayerfully consider whether you should share what you wrote with your son. Regardless of how much you wish to share, be sure to tell him that it's important to you to leave a legacy of faith to him and others.

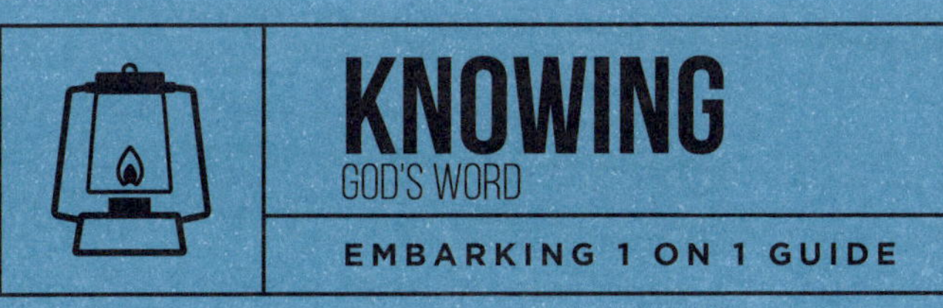

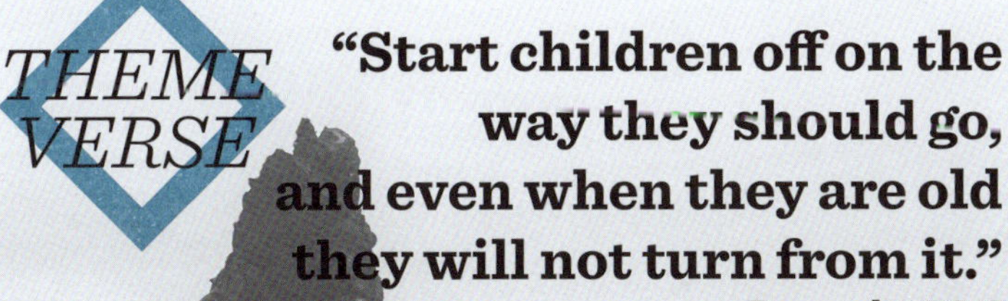

SAY

This is an important verse for our Manhood Journey! It's one of the main reasons we're embarking on this adventure together. My hope for you is that you start your life journey the way you should go, and I pray you'll never turn away from it.

Work together on memorizing this verse. Particularly if your son is younger, you might use a translation such as the New Living Translation, which is easier to read and remember:

"Direct your children onto the right path, and when they are older, they will not leave it" (NLT).

Let's both take a moment to write this verse on the next page in our Manhood Journey Notebooks.

After you both are done, say,

Go ahead and read out loud the verse you just wrote in your notebook. Writing something down and then saying it out loud helps us memorize things.

The Bible calls this practice "hiding God's Word in our hearts" (Psalm 119:11). When we have God's words hidden away in our minds and hearts, they help us live his way all our lives. We are also building up a library of wisdom in our brains so that when we need to remember what God says on a particular topic, we can recall it even when we don't have a Bible readily available.

One of the best ways to memorize a Bible verse is to break it down into smaller chunks and memorize each section before putting it all together. So you might break this verse down this way:

1. Start children off...
2. in the way they should go...
3. and even when they are old...
4. they will not turn from it

Begin with #1 and repeat it several times out loud until you've got it. That's the easiest part. Then work on #2 and when you have it, say both 1 and 2 together. Keep going until you have the whole verse memorized.

Do you understand what this verse means?

Discuss what the verse implies for you as you go through the Manhood Journey together. Here is some important background information on this verse for you, Dad:

"Start children off" is translated as:

"train up a child" in the New King James Version

"teach a youth" in the Holman Christian Standard Bible

"direct your children" in the New Living Translation

Any way it's translated, it means that you as a parent have an indispensible role in pointing your kids in the right direction.

What is "the way they should go"? You will discuss that with your son as you dig deeper in just a moment, but for now, realize there is a way God wants your son to go; your job is to know both God and your son well enough to, over time, help your son understand "the way he should go"—not necessarily the way you want him to go. This is vital! Like Abraham, you may need to surrender your own will and desires for your son (Genesis 22). Surrender him and your own plans for his life over to God.

By the way, "they will not depart from it" does not come with an iron-clad, 100% money-back guarantee that your son will never have doubts or even wander from his faith. The story Jesus told about the prodigal son in Luke 15:11-32 proves that. This is a proverb, not a prophecy! So what's this verse saying? It means that the investment you are making now will bear fruit. What he is learning from you—both your words and your actions— will be an internal part of him for as long as he lives. Your son has free will, of course, and will make his own decisions as he matures. Right now you have the opportunity to instill into him what is most important: a relationship with his heavenly Father.

DIGGING DEEPER

How do you know "the way you should go"?

TIPS

Don't worry about trying to get to the "right" answer. The verses and discussion below will help you get to the answer.

Read or ask your son to read Ephesians 6:4.

Focus your attention on the second part of this verse.

SAY

Your mom and I take our responsibility to bring you up "in the training and instruction of the Lord" very seriously. That's one of the reasons we're doing Manhood Journey together. God knows the way you should go, so Mom and I want to point you in his direction.

How does this verse help you answer the question we just discussed, "How do you know the way you should go?"

The key phrase is "of the Lord." We need to hear from God our Creator about the way we should go.

God's Word, the Bible, contains "the training and instruction of the Lord." (See also Psalm 119:9; 2 Timothy 3:14-17.)

God created you and has a purpose for you. (Read Psalm 139:13-16 and Ephesians 2:10, especially with an older boy.) God created everything that exists, so he knows how things are supposed to work. God gave us the Bible to show us the principles for living a godly life.

Use a map, GPS device or app, or compass as an illustration. Show it to your son, and, if necessary, show him how it works.

How is the Bible like this [map/GPS/compass]?

If we're going on a trip somewhere we've never been before, how does the [map/GPS/compass] help us get there?

If we keep the [map/GPS/compass] in the glove compartment of the car, what do you think will happen?

SAY

As we embark on our journey to manhood, God knows the way to go and he has shown us the way in his Word, the Bible. We'll talk more about the Bible, as well as prayer, in two weeks. For now, let's look at two more Bible passages together.

Read or ask your son to read Psalm 78:1-7.

Why would it have been important for the people to pass on their stories and traditions to the next generation?

For one thing, they did not have books and computers as we do today, so they passed on their history and their faith through their spoken words.

What do you think would happen if we never learned from the generations before us?

How do you think it can make you a better, more godly man by learning from me—from the wise decisions as well as the mistakes I've made in life?

Read or ask your son to read Luke 2:41-52.

Background: Every Jewish male was required to go to Jerusalem three times a year for the important festivals. Jesus was 12 and considered in that culture to be almost an adult, so he may have spent at least some of his time in Jerusalem apart from his parents. The people traveled in large caravans with relatives and neighbors; usually the women traveled together with the children and the men traveled separately, so Jesus could have been in either group.

We know very little about Jesus between the ages of two (Matt. 2:11, 16) and twelve. As with most Jewish boys, he probably spent much of his time with his dad in his carpentry shop, learning his trade.

What were Jesus' priorities (Big Rocks) as a 12-year-old boy?

Point to verse 49—he wanted to be with his heavenly Father and he liked being in a place where he could learn more about and discuss his faith. By the way, the translation of "in my Father's house" from the original language can also mean "in the things of my Father."

Also point to verses 51 and 52 and ask what other Big Rocks were part of Jesus' life.

SAY

In many ways, Jesus was an ordinary 12-year-old boy, but he was also much more than ordinary. His parents knew he was God's Son, the Messiah. Yet, as verse 51 says, Jesus was obedient to his parents.

What does this teach you about why you should be obedient to your parents?

Jesus is our model in all things in life (Phil. 2:1-3). Though he was God in the flesh, he still honored his earthly parents (see Phil. 2:6-7). Also, while Jesus was like us in every way (Heb. 2:17), he did not ever sin (Heb. 4:15), so he honored his earthly father and mother as the Bible commands.

The Bible is silent about the next 18 years of Jesus' life, except for this summary from Luke in verse 52. How would you describe Jesus' manhood journey?

SAY

Much of our Manhood Journey will be about you learning from me as your dad, the same way I learned lessons from my dad. But, more importantly, I think we'll both learn many lessons about life from our heavenly Father as we study and apply his Word together each week.

EVEN DEEPER

Joel 1:3
Psalm 71:17-18
Deuteronomy 6:7
Psalm 119:9
1 Corinthians 14:20

In Luke 2, we saw that the 12-year-old Jesus grew in wisdom and stature, and in favor with God and man. Years later, as the apostle Paul reflected on the things Jesus was known for, he talked about Jesus' humility and said he took on the very nature of a servant (Phil. 2:3, 7), and he said we should model ourselves after him.

What will you do this week that will require you to humble yourself and serve someone else?

Dad, you go first, unless your son immediately has an idea. Try to make this more than just a simple act of service. The idea is that it will take some humility (making yourself less, putting aside pride) on your part. In case your son can't come up with something, have a few ideas ready: doing something nice for a sibling, serving a neighbor, or sending an anonymous, encouraging letter to a teacher, for instance. Again, make this act of humble service a secret just between the two of you.

Write your decisions in your Manhood Journey Notebooks.

TALKING
WITH GOD

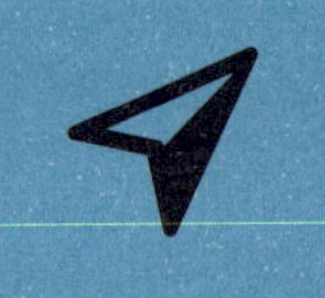

EMBARKING 1 ON 1 GUIDE

Close your time by praying for your son. Pray specifically for something he has going on this week at school, in a sport or other activity, with a friend, or something else. Keep it short and simple! Here's a starter:

Father, thank you for my son(s), _______. Thank you that we have an opportunity to sit down and talk about such important things. Lord, I ask that as he goes through his week, that you be with him and give him strength, as he . . . [mention some of the things he'll be doing].

EMBARKING
WEEK 3

RELYING ON
THE COMPASS

A WORD TO DAD

This week, you will focus on the first Big Rock: trusting God. As dads, we are models for our sons, and nothing that we model is more important in life than this one. Your words and actions are important, but what's even more vital is your own heart. Take a moment before meeting with your son to use the following verses to reflect on your heart.

> *"The LORD does not look at the things people look at. People look at the outward appearance, but the LORD looks at the heart" (1 Sam. 16:7).*
>
> *"Trust in the LORD with all your heart and lean not on your own understanding; in all your ways submit to him, and he will make your paths straight" (Prov. 3:5-6).*
>
> *"Above all else, guard your heart, for everything you do flows from it" (Prov. 4:23).*

Continue your time of reflection by reading and meditating on Psalm 139. Prayerfully focus on verse 23: "Search me, God, and know my heart; test me and know my anxious thoughts."

Journal in your Manhood Journey Notebook any thoughts or convictions you have as you meditate on these Scriptures.

Your heart is important, but this doesn't mean perfection! What's most vital is that you enter into this Manhood Journey with your son asking God to change your heart, help you guard your heart, and make you a man after his own heart (1 Sam. 13:14).

Take your son out to eat this week to discuss the questions under "A Matter of Trust." Be sure to take your Manhood Journey Notebooks with you. Let your son pick the restaurant (within reason, of course!). On the drive there, use some of the following questions to talk about trust:

• Do you trust me to drive us to the restaurant safely? Why or why not?

• Do you trust the other drivers not to run into us? What gives you reason to trust them?

•Why do you think it's a really good idea to always wear our seatbelts?

• Why did you pick the restaurant we're going to?

• What makes you trust the people who cook the food?

• Do you automatically trust other people or do people have to earn your trust? Why?

GROUP SESSION REVIEW

Take a few minutes to talk about the group meeting. If you didn't talk about it during the meeting, tell him about a time in your life when you didn't trust God and things turned out badly.

Did you have any questions about trust that you weren't able to bring up during the meeting?

You don't need to answer all these questions up front; your discussion around the Bible will be good follow-up to these opening questions.

How much do you trust God with your future?

How can I help you trust God more?

How can I help you trust me more?

KNOWING
GOD'S WORD

EMBARKING 1 ON 1 GUIDE

THEME VERSE

"Trust in the LORD with all your heart and lean not on your own understanding."
Proverbs 3:5

Memorize just verse 5 with younger sons. With older sons or any who are good at memorizing, add verse 6: "In all your ways submit to him, and he will make your paths straight."

Write both verses at the top of a new page in each of your Manhood Journey Notebooks.

Even if you only memorized verse 5, include verse 6 in your discussion.

SAY

Trust in this verse literally means to lie face down, totally helpless.

Have your son lie face down on the ground with his arms by his sides.

How do you feel right now? Strong and able to defend yourself or pretty helpless?

SAY

This is how the Bible is describing us when it comes to our need to trust God. We're basically helpless and need his power and strength.

Read or ask your son to read Proverbs 28:26.

This verse says to trust in God with all your heart. Is it even possible to trust God half heartedly?

There is no right answer. It's really a matter of perspective. The purpose of the question is to get your son to think through this. In the verse, "heart" is used figuratively to refer to a person's emotions, intellect, and will; it is the center of everything we are. "All your heart," then, means with everything you are.

What does God promise to people who trust him and submit to (obey) him?

DIGGING DEEPER

Use your Manhood Journey Notebooks for the following discussion. As you draw the following illustration in your notebook, instruct your son to follow along in his own notebook, drawing what you draw but with his own labels.

On a new page in the notebook, draw three large circles in a row or column. Place a stick chair in the center of each circle.

example:

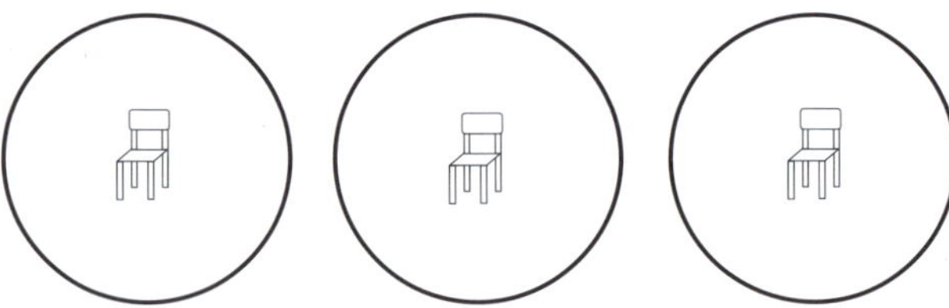

SAY

This circle represents your life and everything in it. The chair represents a throne.

Write inside the borders of the first circle some of the big and little rocks in your life, all the things that are part of your daily life. For now, leave out God. You'll add him in a moment.

Do the same for your circle. Some of the things in your circles will include family members, your job, his schooling, friends, sports and other activities, and so forth. Think about all the things you must "manage" in your life. Prod him to add cleaning his room, a collection he has, his phone, Internet usage, and so forth.

When you've filled up the inner edges of the first circle, copy those same things into the second and third circles; abbreviate if you want.

SAY

Whatever or whomever you place at the center, on the throne, is the one who controls all the other things in the circle. (You might draw lines from the center to the items inside the circle.) The main questions are:

• What or who is on the throne of your life?
• Who is in control?
• Whom do you trust most to manage your life?

Point to where you would place God in the circle.

Before he writes it down, say,

You can live life in three different ways. The first way (circle 1) is with God totally outside your life.

Write God on the outside of circle 1.

**What kind of people live with God
totally outside their lives?**

His answers may vary from non-Christians or unbelievers to atheists. Then, on the throne, write Self.

SAY

In this circle, self is in control. This person is making himself the King or Lord of his life. They probably say things like, "This is MY life."

Move on to the second circle.

The second way that many people live is with God in their lives, but only in their lives, not at the center.

Write God inside the inner edge of the circle alongside some of the other rocks.

SAY

In this picture, God is equal to all the other things we have in our lives. Many people live like this. God is just another object or activity, equal to everything else. God is only a religious activity, the same as all the other activities and interests in the person's life. . . .

Where do you think self is in this circle ?

Self is still on the throne, still in control of this person's life.

Finally, move on to the third circle.

Where do you think God is in this circle?

SAY

God is on the throne in this circle. He is King; he is Lord of this person's life. This person trusts God to be in control. When this person makes decisions about all the other things in his life, he says, as Jesus did, "Not my will, but yours, God, be done."

Self is no longer on the throne. We take a backseat to Jesus.

What circle do you think best represents your life ?

This is a great opportunity to be humble and honest with your son. You might share, in a way that would be helpful to him, an area where you have struggled to keep God at the center.

Sometimes we desire to live in the third circle, and that desire is important, but instead of trusting God completely, we take control. This is a lifelong battle for us as Christ followers.

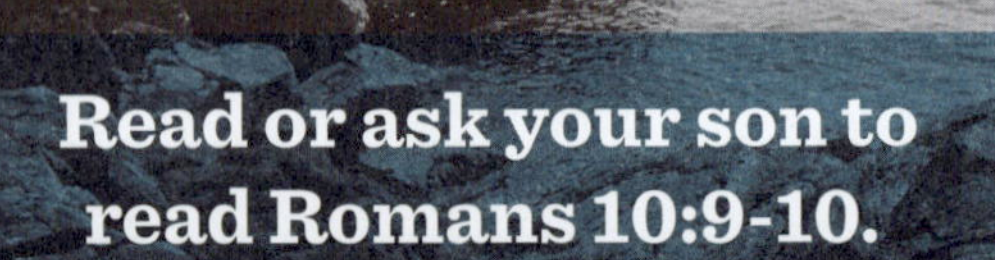

Read or ask your son to read Romans 10:9-10.

What do these verses tell you about living in the third circle?

Look at the phrase, "Jesus is Lord." That means Jesus is on the throne of our lives. The first place we trust him is with our future. We trust that he died and then God raised him from the dead to forgive us of our sins and give us eternal life.

This is a wonderful opportunity to talk to your son about what it means to trust Jesus for salvation.

If your son has already trusted Christ, reaffirm that decision now.

If he hasn't, prayerfully consider leading him to accept Jesus as his Savior and Lord of his life. Follow up that decision by talking with him about what this means and being immersed into Christ (see Romans 6:3-8 and other passages about baptism).

This may also be a great time to share with your son the story about how you came to trust Jesus as your Savior and Lord. If you have not made that decision yet, perhaps you have the incredible opportunity, along with your son, to trust him now! If you need help, don't hesitate to ask your group leader or a minister from your church.

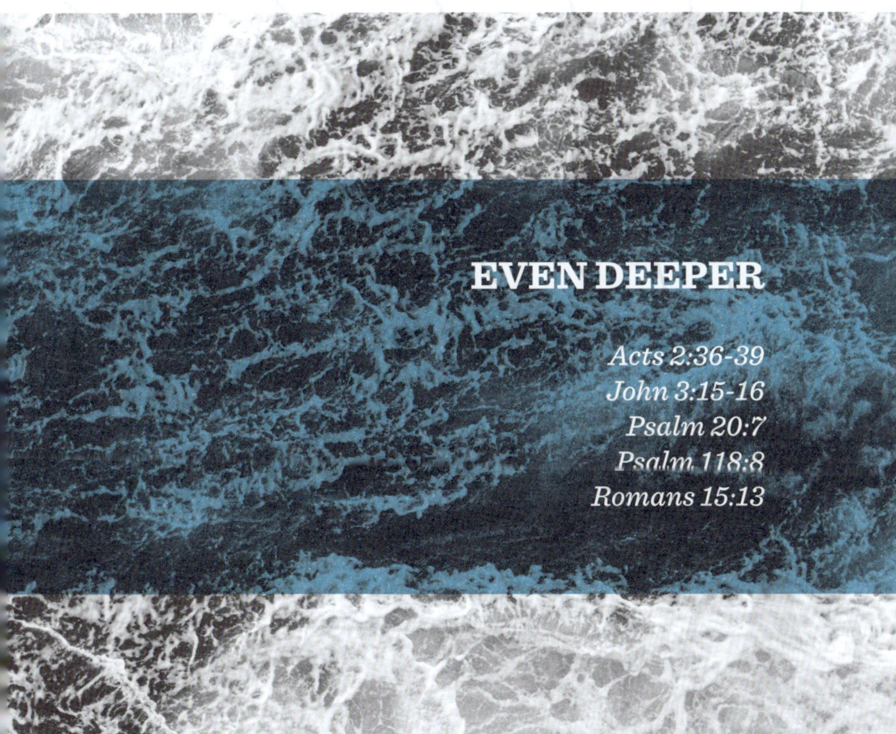

SERVING
OTHERS

EMBARKING 1 ON 1 GUIDE

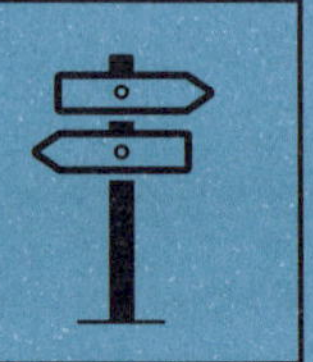

Look again at the page in your Manhood Journey Notebooks with the three circles.

Do you have friends at school, in the neighborhood, or through your sports or other activities who have not yet trusted Jesus as Lord and Savior?

Your friends are part of your life; they're in your circle. With God on the throne of your life, what do you think you should do?

How would you pray for them?

Would you tell them about your decision to follow Jesus as your Lord and Savior?

SAY

In your Manhood Journey Notebook, write the names of one, two, or three of your friends who do not yet know or trust Jesus as Lord and Savior.

As your son writes down these names in his notebook, write the names of 1-3 of your friends who are not yet Christ followers in your own notebook. Share the names with each other and how you know each of these people. Then commit to pray for these people each day over the next week.

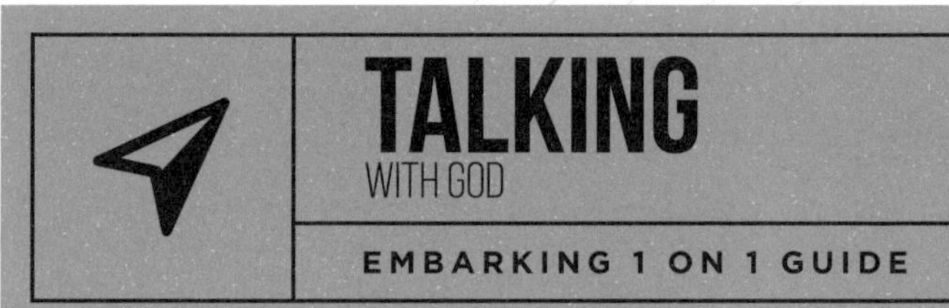

Close your time together with a simple prayer such as this:

God, we ask you to work in these friends' lives and to draw them to yourself. We want you at the center of our lives as our Lord and we know you are in control of all things. Amen.

EMBARKING
WEEK 4
SEEKING GUIDANCE
ALONG THE WAY

A WORD TO DAD

This week you are discussing the vitality of seeking God's guidance through the Bible and prayer. These are foundation stones for your relationship with God. As with any relationship—with your wife, children, and co-workers, for instance—regular, clear communication is crucial. When we read God's Word, we have the opportunity to hear from him and when we pray we have the privilege to speak to our Creator and Savior.

Before meeting with your son, take some time to pray for him and his spiritual development. First, read Colossians 1:9-10. Use this as a template for your prayer.

Imagine your relationship with your son on his twenty-first birthday. On that day, what would you like to say to him? If you are not already doing so, start today to pray daily for your wife, son, and other children. May you be able to write your son a letter on his twenty-first birthday that reflects Paul's words to the Colossian church:

I have not stopped praying for you since [the day you were born or today's date: ________]. I ask God to give you complete knowledge of his will and to give you spiritual wisdom and understanding. Then the way you live will always honor and please the Lord, and your life will produce every kind of good fruit. All the while, you will grow as you learn to know God better and better.

Before meeting with your son, think about something you did as a kid with your dad, or if your dad was unavailable, with a grandfather, uncle, teacher, coach, or some other father figure. If you can, do something similar with your son. This might be something like fishing, tossing ball, or playing chess, for instance.

Use this as an opener to tell your son about this father figure, what he was like, and what he taught you. Share how he helped you be the man you are today.

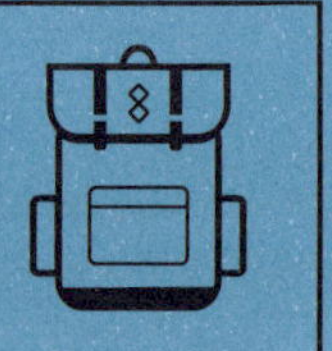

BUILDING
OUR RELATIONSHIP

EMBARKING 1 ON 1 GUIDE

GROUP SESSION REVIEW

• What did you learn about the Big Rocks of Knowing God's Word and prayer?

• In what ways do you think the Bible is like an instruction manual from God? How are they different?

• Why is it critical for our lives as Christ followers to read our Bibles and pray?

• What does it mean to you to live according to God's Word?

In Matthew 6:5-15, Jesus taught his disciples to pray. Read this passage together.

Read or paraphrase the following paragraphs as you look together at this Bible passage:

SAY

Verses 9b-13 are sometimes called the "Lord's Prayer," which is often recited in churches. But Jesus wasn't teaching his followers a prayer to recite; he was teaching them how to pray (see v. 5). He was modeling for them how to talk to our Father in heaven.

First, look at verses 5-8. What did Jesus say about our attitude and heart when we come to the Father in prayer?

SAY

Notice how Jesus started with **worship** (v. 9). When we begin talking to God and realize who he is, it's natural for us to begin by worshiping him!

Note also the **goal** of prayer. Jesus' goal as he prayed was, "your will be done" (v. 10), not "here's my list of what I want you to do for me, God."

Next, Jesus **asked the Father for what he needed** (v. 11); Jesus **trusted** the Father to provide what he needed.

Jesus taught his disciples to ask the Father for **forgiveness** (v. 12); this includes **confessing** our faults to him. But he also mentioned an important aspect of this: We must also **forgive others** who hurt us.

Finally, Jesus asked the Father for something we all need to continually ask God for: to **protect us when we are tempted** (v. 13). Satan is real and wants us to give in to his evil schemes. We need God's power and wisdom every day as we fight temptation and evil.

Use this outline to teach your son to pray in his own words and from his own heart:

A. Come to God with the right attitude and heart.

B. Begin by worshiping God.

C. Have the right goal for your prayer.

D. Ask for what you need, and trust God.

E. Confess your sins and ask for forgiveness.

F. Forgive others who have hurt you.

G. Ask God to protect you and help you when tempted.

Note that this is just an outline, not a formula or an agenda you must follow point by point. Teach him how to simply have an honest conversation with his heavenly Father.

KNOWING
GOD'S WORD

EMBARKING 1 ON 1 GUIDE

"Get wisdom, get understanding; do not forget my words or turn away from them."
Proverbs 4:5

SAY

Later, we'll discuss the whole chapter of Proverbs 4. For now, let's work together on memorizing this key verse.

Write this verse at the top of a new page in each of your Manhood Journey Notebooks.

Where do you think real wisdom and understanding come from? What is their ultimate source?

We receive some wisdom from parents, grandparents, and others who have more life experience, of course. But ultimately, the source of true wisdom is God.

Wisdom is not the same as intelligence or being smart in school.

DIGGING DEEPER

Be sure to have a Bible for yourself as well as one for your son (or each son).

In your own Bibles, read Proverbs 4. As you read it, underline or highlight any words, phrases, or verses that stand out to either of you.

SAY

King Solomon wrote these words, and we can imagine him sitting down with his sons, like we're doing now, and sharing this wisdom with them. Solomon's father was King David, the "man after God's heart." Solomon was blessed to have a godly, even if imperfect, father, and Solomon's sons had the privilege of receiving this wisdom passed down from generation to generation.

Let's look at the verses we each underlined or highlighted and discuss why those parts stood out to us.

Go through the passage, talking about what you each under-lined and why.

According to this passage, what is the value of having wisdom? In other words, how does having wisdom benefit us?

If you want to drill down deeper into the benefits of wisdom, see Proverbs 8:11; 9:12; 16:16; 19:8, 11; and 28:26.

What is the dad's responsibility in seeking and passing on wisdom?
What is the son's responsibility?

Let's focus in on verses 23-27.

In a physical battle, why is it critical
to guard your heart?

How about spiritually?
What does it mean to guard your heart?

Why is that important?

Fold your arms in front of your chest so that they form the letter X.

SAY

It's vital that we guard our hearts against anything or anyone that would want to corrupt them. This is also the sign in sign language for "love." I just want you to know that I love you and I want you to be sure that you carefully and courageously guard your heart. Everything you do flows out of it.

What do these verses say we should do to stay on God's path of wisdom?

The most obvious thing we can do is practice the disciplines of Bible study and prayer. They are our way to know God and his path for our lives.

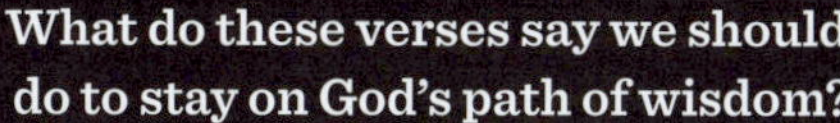

Read or have your son read aloud 2 Timothy 3:14-17.

Paul was writing to his "son" in the faith, Timothy, a young man Paul discipled.

How did Paul describe the Bible?

"God-breathed" means that it is inspired by God. Humans like the apostle Paul wrote it down, but God gave them the words.

What is God's Word useful for?

EVEN DEEPER

Psalm 119:1-8
Psalm 119:9-16
Psalm 119:33-40
Psalm 119:57-64
Psalm 119:105-112

Note that Psalm 119, like most psalms, is one long prayer.

Read Colossians 4:2-6.

What will you do this week to
be devoted to prayer?

What time of each day do you
want to devote to spending time
with God and praying?

TALKING
WITH GOD

EMBARKING 1 ON 1 GUIDE

Open back to the page in your Manhood Journey Notebooks where you each wrote the names of friends who are not yet Christ followers. Close your time in prayer. Use the following prayer prompts to guide you:

SAY

- Heavenly Father, we know you are present with us and that you are all-powerful. We praise you for who you are.

- We want your will to be done through our lives.

- We ask you to forgive us for when we've failed you.

- Guard our hearts against temptation and evil.

- We ask you to open doors this week to serve our friends and tell them about you.

- Help us share your message clearly.

- Give us wisdom and grace, especially in the way we treat others this week.

EMBARKING
WEEK 5
ENCOUNTERING OTHERS ALONG
THE JOURNEY

A WORD TO DAD

You have entered into this Manhood Journey with your son in large part because you care about him and the path he will take into manhood. You know that his relationships have a profound impact on the way he will go and how critical it is that he wisely chooses good friends along the way. Men who have reared their kids into young adults will tell you that you can have a powerful influence on your children's choices, but, short of locking them in your house with no TV or Internet access, you cannot have complete control. That's hard for some moms and dads. This is where prayer for your children and a trust in our all-powerful God is essential. No matter how young your children are now, be sure to pray for them daily.

If you are part of a Manhood Journey group, you have surrounded yourself with other dads who have the same priorities as you do. The Bible passages you study with your son are as important for you as they are for him. You probably already know this, but you need other men who will be there to reach down to help you up when you fall. You need men of good character in your life to encourage you, support you, pray for you, and sharpen you, and you need to be that kind of godly man for others as well.

Before your meeting, spend time with your son asking him about his friends. Why are they friends? What do they have in common? Does he think they are good friends? Tell him about a good friend you had when you were his age. Give your son an insight into your childhood and choices. How did that friend impact your life? Are you still friends today or did the friendship change as you grew into manhood? This is a time to tell stories (helpful stories!), not to judge or make a point.

GROUP SESSION REVIEW

If you are part of a Manhood Journey group, talk in more depth about the university experiment story. If you are not in a group, read the following story:

SAY

There was a university experiment where a psychology professor conducted a test of peer pressure on various students. He created a classroom where nine students were aware of what the experiment was about, and he rotated in a tenth one who had no idea that everyone else was playing along with the professor.

The teacher drew two lines on the board, one long and one short. He then asked the class which line was shorter.

The nine students who had been prepared ahead of time were told to raise their hand when the professor pointed to the correct line, but they all eventually changed their minds after repeatedly being asked if they were sure.

As each new student was brought in, he or she watched everyone else give a wrong answer, and most of the time, this student went along with the crowd, even though it was obvious which line was longer.

What the professor found was that the assurance of the group and the loneliness of standing out were too much for the students to handle.

Why do you think the tenth student went along with the crowd even though he knew the answer was wrong?

When have you ever seen something like this happen—where people knew something was wrong but they went along with the crowd anyway?

What do you think it takes to go against the crowd?

You might tell the story of Shadrach, Meshach, and Abednego from Daniel 3. When the entire population fell down to worship the image of gold as commanded by the king, these three godly men refused. They would not go along with the crowd even with the threat from the king of being thrown into a blazing furnace. They trusted their God and lived by his principles of right and wrong.

WHAT WOULD YOU DO?

Play a game of "What would you do if . . . ?" Here are some examples (use these as age-appropriate for your son):

WHAT WOULD YOU DO IF . . .

- friends ask you to play "Truth or Dare" with no restrictions?

- a classmate asks if he can look at your test or project?

- some kids in the neighborhood make fun of you because you're a Christian?

- everyone else on your team, including the coaches, are going along with a scheme to cheat in order to win a big game?

- you go on a school trip and stay in a hotel room with other boys and several of them turn on a TV channel or go to a web site that you know you should not be looking at?

Let your son ask you some "What would you do if . . . ?" questions as well!

KNOWING
GOD'S WORD

EMBARKING 1 ON 1 GUIDE

THEME VERSE

"Iron sharpens iron, so one man sharpens another."
Proverbs 27:17,
New American Standard Bible

This should be an easy verse to memorize. If you'd like to add other verses or select one that is a bit more challenging or more appropriate for your son, use Ecclesiastes 4:9; Proverbs 13:20; or 1 Corinthians 15:33.

As usual, write the verse at the top of a new page in each of your Manhood Journey Notebooks.

Regardless of the verse you choose to memorize, discuss its meaning and talk about examples of how you would live it out.

DIGGING DEEPER

SAY

Today, we're going to look at some Bible verses in a machine-gun-type tempo. We won't spend very much time on each one. The goal today is to see what the Bible says about whom we choose as friends and why we develop friendships. For each Bible passage, we'll answer one basic question:

What does this verse teach you about building relationships?

Proverbs 13:20
Proverbs 12:26
Proverbs 22:24-25
1 Corinthians 15:33
Genesis 2:18
Psalm 68:6a
Proverbs 27:17
Ecclesiastes 4:9-10
John 15:13-15
1 John 1:3

After reading these verses, what does the
Bible say about friendships?

What kinds of friends should we choose?

How do true friends help us to be better followers of Christ?

SAY

In our Manhood Journey Notebooks, let's both write down what we learned about biblical friendships today.

We need strong, godly friendships in order to grow and live as followers of Christ. But it's not all about us! We should be humble, like Jesus, and put other people above ourselves. Like Jesus, we are to live the lifestyle of a servant (rf. Phil. 2:1-8).

Use one of these two examples of how our friendships create opportunities for us to serve.

What's the purpose of the huddle in a football game? (To get the team on the same page, plan the next play, encourage one another, and so forth.)

Does a team win the game by staying in the huddle? (No. You have to break the huddle to carry out your mission; to win the game.)

What's the purpose of a platoon of soldiers on a battle field?

They develop strong friendships with one another as they train and go over strategies together, but their purpose is to defeat the enemy they're fighting. As they do, they have each others' backs and never leave a brother behind.

Read Romans 12:3-21.

How do these verses say we should think of ourselves?

Especially look at verses 3, 5, and 10.

SAY

Let's each write Romans 12:3-21 (just the reference, not all the verses!), in our Manhood Journey Notebooks, and then list everything this passage instructs us as Christ followers to do.

Take your time looking through the verses and compiling your list. Depending on how you count them, there are 25-30 commands for us to follow here, and they all have to do with how we live in and through our Christian community. If your son doesn't understand a particular instruction, take a moment and talk about that one.

EVEN DEEPER

Acts 2:42-47
Ephesians 2:10
1 Peter 4:10-11
1 Peter 3:8-9
1 Peter 3:13-15

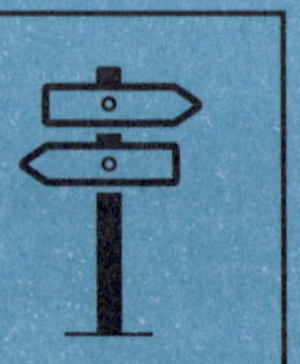

Look at the lists you compiled in your Manhood Journey Notebooks from Romans 12.

SAY

Let's evaluate how well we're each following those instructions.

Which ones do you think you're doing really well? (Mark those with a smiley face in your notebooks.)

Which ones do you need to get better at doing? (Mark those with an upward arrow to symbolize a need to grow.)

Dad, be sure to do the same exercise for
yourself in your notebook!

Now, pick one area from your list in which
you want to grow the most. Circle it in your
notebook. As you pray this week, ask God to
give you strength, wisdom, and opportunities
to serve in that way.

Think of one or two things you can do this
next week that shows love to others by
serving them. Will the person you serve be
someone in our family, someone at school
(or work, for you), or somebody else?

Write down the name(s) and what you can do
in your notebook.

Look back again at the names of people who are not yet Christ followers that you wrote down in your Manhood Journey Notebooks at the end of Session 3.

Have you had any interaction or discussions with these friends this past week?

Tell your son about conversations you've had with your friends.

TALKING
WITH GOD

EMBARKING 1 ON 1 GUIDE

Close your time together in prayer. Use the following prayer starter:

Father, thank you for our time together studying your Word and talking today. We lift up our friends to you [mention their names] and we ask you to give us opportunities this week to serve other people in your name. We want you to receive all the credit and glory as we serve others and you. Amen.

EMBARKING
WEEK 6
WE HAVE EMBARKED
WHERE TO NEXT?

A WORD TO DAD

Congratulations! You've made a huge investment into your son(s) and yourself as you have embarked on this Manhood Journey together. When we step out of our comfort zones and faithfully invest what God has given us, he responds, "Well done, good and faithful servant!" What an honor it is to hear your Creator and Master say those words to you. But there's even more! He says, "You have been faithful with a few things; I will put you in charge of many things. Come and share your master's happiness!" (Matthew 25:21).

"Embarking" is just the beginning of your Manhood Journey together. God promises that when you are loyal in handling smaller responsibilities, he will entrust you with more. (That's a great child-rearing principle, by the way!)

"Come and share your master's happiness!" God celebrates this victory with you, but he also calls you into a partnership with him. You are not rearing your son on your own. You have a partnership with God, your wife, and others in your Christian community.

Don't forget the biblical principle: "a man reaps what he sows" (Gal. 6:7). So keep going. "Let us not become weary in doing good, for at the proper time we will reap a harvest if we do not give up" (v. 9).

Do something special with your son this week to celebrate the completion of the Embarking module of Manhood Journey. Go to a guy movie, go-carting, or on a bike ride together, or do something else he would enjoy. Spend time simply reflecting on the last five weeks of the Manhood Journey. You can use some of the conversation questions under the Group Session Review in this session.

GROUP SESSION REVIEW

If you're part of a Manhood Journey small group, continue the discussion from the group session in regard to reviewing this module and continuing with another module.

As always, be sure to share what you are thinking as well!

- What did you think overall about the first module of Manhood Journey?

- What did you most enjoy about the study?

- Was there anything you'd want to do differently?

- Are you excited about continuing with the next module that we decided on? Why or why not?

Whether or not you have been a part of a Manhood Journey small group, discuss these two questions with your son:

Do you remember the 5 Big Rocks?
What are they?

Which Big Rock do you think you
still need or want to work on?

RE-VERSES

SAY

Let's look back in our Manhood Journey Notebooks at the theme verses we've memorized during the last five weeks. Let's see how well you remember each one.

Spend time going over them again. Working together to recall them now will help to cement them in your memories for the future.

Use some or all of these questions to talk about the memory verses:

Which memory verse is the most meaningful to you?

Why did you choose that one?
Why is it significant to you?

Do you find yourself thinking about this
verse at different times during the week?
When? What are the situations?

SAY

We have one more verse to memorize in this
module. This verse and the others we'll discuss
this week deal with wise planning, an important
topic as we move forward in our Manhood
Journey and in life.

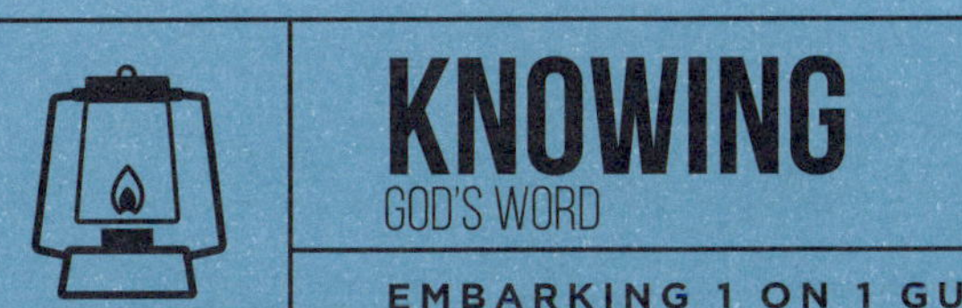

Write this verse at the top of a new page in each of your Manhood Journey Notebooks and work on memorizing it.

SAY

What's does it mean to commit whatever you do to the Lord? It means we do what we do for God, not for ourselves or others; and we depend on him for success. A similar verse is in Colossians 3:23-24:

Whatever you do, work at it with all your heart, as working for the Lord, not for men, since you know that you will receive an inheritance from the Lord as a reward. It is the Lord Christ you are serving (NIV, 1984).

DIGGING DEEPER

Today we will spend less time digging deeper into God's Word, but it's no less important!

Look up and discuss the following verses. Discuss what they say about having goals and making plans.

Proverbs 21:5
Philippians 3:14
Proverbs 19:21

What do you learn about having goals and making plans in these passages?

The Bible shows us that wise planning is essential in life, but the main question is, "whose goals and plans should we be making and living out?"

> **What can we apply from these verses in relation to our future plans and goals for Manhood Journey?**

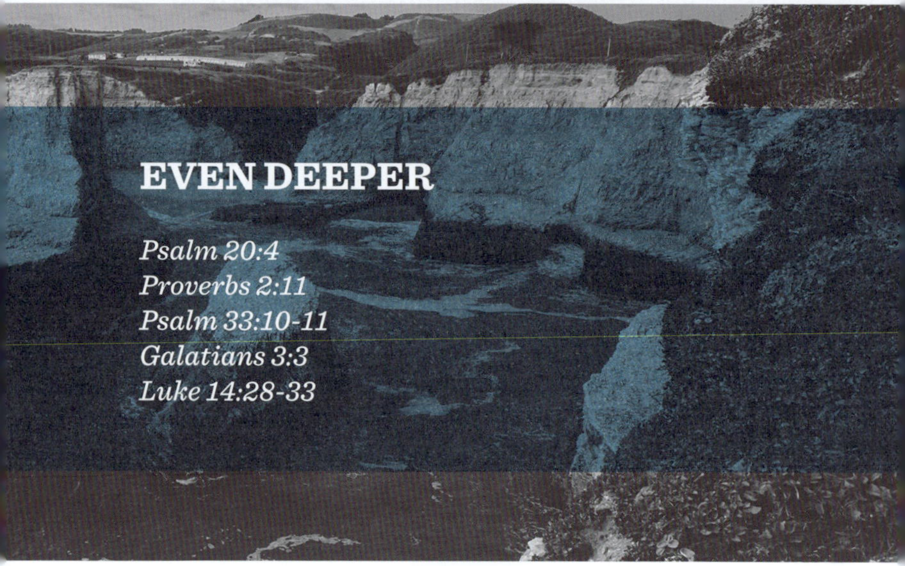

EVEN DEEPER

Psalm 20:4
Proverbs 2:11
Psalm 33:10-11
Galatians 3:3
Luke 14:28-33

Use the discussion questions from the "Digging Deeper" section to continue this conversation.

Let's look back at how we've loved others through acts of service, sharing our faith, and praying for others over the last five weeks.

Did you have a favorite way that you loved and ministered to others?

Did any give you a sense of joy as you humbly served other people?

Have there been any times as you served others that you felt like this is why God made you? How?

Were any of the ways you've served others harder for you than others? Why do you think they felt harder?

During the past five weeks, what changes in yourself have you noticed?

TIPS

Be sure to tell your son what changes in his faith, character, and maturity you've noticed. This is a great opportunity to build him up.

How have you seen God work through
your acts of service, prayers, or
sharing your faith?

Do you sense God leading you to follow up on
anything you've done, said, or prayed? If so, what?

If you are part of a Manhood Journey small group, use this question:

Between now and when our group starts
the next module, how do you want to
continue moving forward? Do you want for
me and you to keep meeting weekly or take
a break?

Pull out the Module Map (on the inside back cover of this guide) Or look at the descriptions of all the modules at www.manhood-journey.org/modules. Talk about what other topics you would like to address in the future.

If you are not in a Manhood Journey small group, use the following discussion points. Use the Module Map or look through the list of modules on the Manhood Journey website (www.manhoodjourney.org) as you discuss:

Which module do you want to work through next?

This could be a great opportunity to start our own Manhood Journey small group. What would you think about exploring that option?

You will find lots of resources and ideas for doing so on the Manhood Journey website under the "Get Started" tab.

TALKING
WITH GOD

EMBARKING 1 ON 1 GUIDE

We'll close our time together by praying for each other. I'll pray for you first, and then you pray for me. OK?

IMPORTANT! Be sure to pray briefly with normal, everyday words and tone of voice. Remember that prayer is a conversation with a personal God.

After you have each prayed briefly for one another, close your time asking God to bring about his purposes through your lives. Dad, lead this prayer with words such as these:

SAY

Heavenly Father, we praise you for who you are. You are powerful. You know everything about us, inside and out. You know how you made us and what you created us to do. You are our King and the Leader of our lives. So we commit whatever we do to you, knowing you will work in and through us. May your will be done! Be with ________ [your son's name] as he seeks to live for you. We pray in the name of Jesus. Amen.

A FINAL WORD TO DAD

Borrow your son's Manhood Journey Notebook and then privately write another note to him on the next empty page. Tell him how proud you are of him for completing this module together. Let him know that you look forward to spending more time together in pursuit of becoming godly men. Write a brief prayer for him, something like, "I pray that you will . . ." Be sure to sign and date it.

Leave his notebook on his pillow before he goes to bed.

CONTINUING A MANHOOD JOURNEY GROUP IS EASY

This kit contains everything you need to begin your journey, including:

• Embarking Group Guide - 6 week discussion on the five key areas of Biblical Manhood

• 1 on 1 Guide for daily actitives and study with your son(s)

• DVD of the introductory videos for the first 6 modules

• (10) Maprochures – an informational brochure/map of the first 6 modules

SAVE 20%
use coupon code: MJEN20

ALSO AVAILABLE

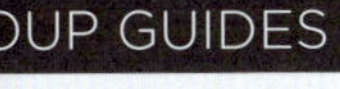

OUP GUIDES

key topics of cal manhood

N 1 GUIDES

aily activities & ssion with your

SHOP AT WWW.MANHOODJOURNEY.ORG